# MY BOOK

JAKE BROWN

# Contents

# 1. The History of Domesticated Rats

The history of domesticated rats dates back to ancient China, where they were kept as pets, bred for food, and used for hunting. It is believed that the first domesticated rats were bred specifically for hunting, as they were much more agile and skilled at catching small prey than their wild counterparts.

Rats were also valued for their meat and fur, and were often kept in large numbers for these purposes. However, in the 18th and 19th centuries, rats began to be kept as pets in Europe.

The first known rat show was held in England in 1901, with over 300 rats competing for prizes. This event marked the beginning of the fancy rat movement, which focused on breeding rats for show and companionship rather than practical purposes.

Throughout the 20th century, rats became increasingly popular as pets in the United States and other parts of the world. However, they also continued to be used in research labs due to their intelligence and ability to be trained to perform tasks.

Despite their long history as domesticated animals, rats still face negative perceptions. In many cultures, they are seen as pests and carriers of disease and are often associated with filth and decay.

However, there has been a growing movement in recent years to promote rats as pets and educate the public on their positive qualities. Rats are social animals that form strong bonds with their owners and are intelligent and playful pets that can learn tricks and even respond to their names.

There are over 60 varieties of domesticated rats, including fancy rats, dumbo rats, hairless rats, rex rats, and more. Each breed has its own unique characteristics and can make an excellent companion for the right owner.

In the following chapters, we will explore the different types of pet rats in more detail and discuss how to properly care for and train them. With the proper knowledge and attention, rats can make fantastic pets and valued family members.

## 2. Wild Rats vs. Domesticated Rats

## Wild Rats vs. Domesticated Rats

Rats are a highly adaptable species that can thrive in various environments. As a result, they can be found worldwide, both in the wild and as domesticated pets. While wild and domesticated rats may look similar, there are some significant differences between the two.

Physical Characteristics

Wild rats are typically larger and more robust than domesticated rats. They have longer, thicker tails, and their fur is often thicker and coarser. Wild rats also tend to have a more elongated, pointed snout and larger, more pronounced ears.

Domesticated rats, on the other hand, are bred for specific traits, such as size, color, and temperament. As a result, they come in a wide range of sizes, colors, and coat types and may have shorter, stubbier tails and more rounded facial features than their wild counterparts.

## Behavior

Wild rats are highly social animals that live in large colonies, often with a complex social hierarchy. They are generally wary of humans and other animals and avoid contact whenever possible.

Domesticated rats, on the other hand, are bred to be more docile and friendly. They are highly social and thrive on interaction with their owners, often forming strong bonds with them.

## Diet

Wild rats are omnivorous and eat almost anything they can find, including fruits, vegetables, grains, and meat. They are also opportunistic scavengers and will eat food scraps and garbage.

On the other hand, domesticated rats are typically fed a diet of commercial rat food supplemented with fresh fruits and vegetables. Some owners also feed their rats insects, such as crickets and mealworms.

## Health

Wild rats are more susceptible to disease than domesticated rats, as they are exposed to a broader range of pathogens in their natural environment. They are also more likely to carry parasites and other pests.

On the other hand, domesticated rats are generally healthier than their wild counterparts, as they are bred in controlled environments and receive regular veterinary care. However, they are still susceptible to certain health issues, such as respiratory infections, tumors, and dental problems.

Conclusion

While wild and domesticated rats may look similar, there are some important differences between the two. Domesticated rats are generally smaller, more docile, and more prone to certain health issues than their wild counterparts. However, with proper care and attention, both wild and domesticated rats can thrive and make excellent companions.

## 3. Why choose a rat as a pet

Rats are often overlooked as pets, but they make wonderful companions for the right person. There are several reasons why rats make great pets, including their social nature, intelligence, and adaptability.

Firstly, rats are highly social animals and thrive on interaction with their owners. They love to play, cuddle, and explore their surroundings. Rats are happiest when they have plenty of stimulation, so providing them with toys, tunnels, and climbing structures is essential. Additionally, rats are highly intelligent and can be taught a variety of tricks, such as fetching, spinning, and even playing basketball.

Secondly, rats are very adaptable and can easily adjust to different living environments. They are relatively low-maintenance pets that require a simple diet of high-quality pellets, fresh water, and occasional treats. Rats are also clean animals that groom themselves regularly, and their feces are small and odorless.

Thirdly, rats have unique personalities that make them incredibly endearing. Each rat has its own quirks, likes, and dislikes. Some rats are very active and outgoing, while others are more relaxed and laid-back. Additionally, rats are very affectionate and form strong bonds with their owners. They love to snuggle and be held, and they will often groom their owners as a sign of affection.

Lastly, rats are relatively long-lived for small pets, with an average lifespan of 2-3 years. This means that owners can form a long-lasting bond with their pet rat and enjoy many years of companionship.

Of course, like any pet, there are some downsides to owning a rat. Rats require regular attention and interaction, which may be difficult for some owners to provide. Additionally, rats are prone to health issues such as respiratory infections and tumors, so owners need to be vigilant about monitoring their pet's health and providing regular veterinary care.

Overall, the many benefits of owning a rat make them a great choice for the right person. With proper care and attention, rats can provide years of companionship and joy.

## 4. The different types of pet rats

Fancy Rats:

These are the most common type of pet rat, and come in a wide variety of colors and patterns. They are typically bred for their docile temperament and make great pets for both children and adults.

Dumbo Rats:

Dumbo rats are a type of fancy rat that have larger, rounder ears that are set lower on their heads. They are known for their sweet and gentle nature, and are often favored by rat enthusiasts.

Hairless Rats:

Hairless rats are a unique breed that lack fur due to a genetic mutation. They have smooth, soft skin and are highly social and affectionate pets. However, they do require special care to protect their sensitive skin.

Rex Rats:

Rex rats have a curly or wavy coat that gives them a unique appearance. They are friendly and intelligent, and are often used in research labs due to their intelligence and ability to be trained.

Siamese Rats:

Siamese rats have a pointed, triangular face and a distinctive dark marking on their nose and around their eyes. They are highly social and affectionate pets, and are known for their playful and energetic personalities.

Black Hooded Rats:

Black hooded rats have a black coat with a distinctive white marking on their chest and around their necks. They are known for their friendly and social personalities, and make great pets for families with children.

Albino Rats:

Albino rats have white fur and pink eyes due to a lack of melanin in their bodies. They are highly social and affectionate pets, but require special care to protect their sensitive eyes from bright light.

Blue Rats:

Blue rats have a distinctive blue-gray coat and are known for their calm and gentle personalities. They make great pets for families with children, as they are both friendly and easy to handle.

Champagne Rats:

Champagne rats have a beige or tan coat and are known for their sweet and affectionate nature. They make great pets for both children and adults.

Chocolate Rats:

Chocolate rats have a brown coat that can range from light to dark in color. They are known for their friendly and social personalities, and make great pets for families with children.

Cinnamon Rats:

Cinnamon rats have a reddish-brown coat and are known for their playful and energetic personalities. They make great pets for both children and adults.

Silver Rats:

Silver rats have a silver-gray coat and are known for their intelligence and affectionate nature. They make great pets for rat enthusiasts who are looking for a more unique pet.

Pearl Rats:

Pearl rats have a white coat with a distinctive gray marking on their heads. They are known for their playful and energetic personalities, and make great pets for families with children.

Fawn Rats:

Fawn rats have a light brown or beige coat and are known for their calm and gentle personalities. They make great pets for both children and adults.

Beige Rats:

Beige rats have a light brown or tan coat and are known for their sweet and affectionate nature. They make great pets for families with children.

Lilac Rats:

Lilac rats have a light purple or lavender coat and are known for their calm and gentle personalities. They make great pets for both children and adults.

Mink Rats:

Mink rats have a brown coat with a distinctive gray undercoat. They are known for their friendly and social personalities, and make great pets for families with children.

Russian Blue Rats:

Russian blue rats have a distinctive blue-gray coat and are known for their

Himalayan Rats:

Himalayan rats have a white coat with dark-colored ears, nose, and feet. They are known for their friendly and curious personalities, and make great pets for rat enthusiasts.

Agouti Rats:

Agouti rats have a brown or grayish-brown coat with a distinctive "salt and pepper" appearance. They are known for their active and curious personalities, and make great pets for both children and adults.

Hooded Rats:

Hooded rats have a colored coat with a distinctive white marking on their head and neck that resembles a hood. They are known for their friendly and social personalities, and make great pets for families with children.

Variegated Rats:

Variegated rats have a coat that is a mix of two or more colors. They are known for their playful and energetic personalities, and make great pets for rat enthusiasts.

Berkshire Rats:

Berkshire rats have a white belly and a dark-colored coat that extends from their head to their tail. They are known for their friendly and curious personalities, and make great pets for both children and adults.

Burmese Rats:

Burmese rats have a golden-brown coat and are known for their affectionate and playful personalities. They make great pets for families with children.

Fox Rats:

Fox rats have a distinctive reddish-brown coat and are known for their friendly and social personalities. They make great pets for both children and adults.

Marten Rats:

Marten rats have a dark-colored coat with a distinctive light-colored undercoat. They are known for their active and curious personalities, and make great pets for rat enthusiasts.

Merle rats:

Merle rats have a marbled or speckled coat with a mix of colors.

Splashed Rats:

Splashed rats have a coat that is mostly white with colored patches or spots. They are known for their social and curious personalities, and make great pets for both children and adults.

Capped Rats:

Capped rats have a colored coat with a distinctive white marking on their head. They are known for their active and playful personalities, and make great pets for rat enthusiasts.

Irish Rats:

Irish rats have a white belly and a colored coat that extends from their head to their tail. They are known for their friendly and social personalities, and make great pets for families with children.

Patched Rats:

Patched rats have a coat that is mostly colored with white patches or spots. They are known for their curious and energetic personalities, and make great pets for both children and adults.

Roan Rats:

Roan rats have a coat that is mostly white with colored hairs mixed in. They are known for their friendly and outgoing personalities, and make great pets for rat enthusiasts.

Satin Rats:

Satin rats have a shiny, silky coat that is available in many different colours. They are known for their gentle and docile personalities, and make great pets for both children and adults.

Chinchilla Rats:

Chinchilla rats have a coat that is light gray or white with a slight blue tint. They are known for their calm and gentle personalities, and make great pets for families with children.

Shadow Rats:

Shadow rats have a dark-coloured coat that is almost black. They are known for their playful and energetic personalities, and make great pets for rat enthusiasts.

Topaz Rats:

Topaz rats have a coat that is a golden-brown color, similar to the gemstone. They are known for their friendly and curious personalities, and make great pets for both children and adults.

Amethyst Rats:

Amethyst rats have a coat that is a deep purple color, similar to the gemstone. They are known for their affectionate and playful personalities, and make great pets for families with children.

Garnet Rats:

Garnet rats have a coat that is a deep red color, similar to the gemstone. They are known for their social and outgoing personalities, and make great pets for rat enthusiasts.

Peridot Rats:

Peridot rats have a coat that is a bright green color, similar to the gemstone. They are known for their active and curious personalities, and make great pets for both children and adults.

Ruby Rats:

Ruby rats have a coat that is a deep red color, similar to the gemstone. They are known for their friendly and affectionate personalities, and make great pets for families with children.

Sapphire Rats:

Sapphire rats have a coat that is a deep blue color, similar to the gemstone. They are known for their playful and social personalities, and make great pets for both children and adults.

Emerald Rats:

Emerald rats have a coat that is a bright green color, similar to the gemstone. They are known for their friendly and active personalities, and make great pets for rat enthusiasts.

Opal Rats:

Opal rats have a coat that is iridescent and reflects many different colors. They are known for their gentle and affectionate personalities, and make great pets for families with children.

Tourmaline Rats:

Tourmaline rats have a coat that is a pink or green color, similar to the gemstone. They are known for their social and curious personalities, and make great pets for rat enthusiasts.

Aquamarine Rats:

Aquamarine rats have a coat that is a light blue color, similar to the gemstone. They are known for their active and playful personalities, and make great pets for both children and adults.

Alexandrite Rats:

Alexandrite rats have a coat that appears to change color in different lighting, similar to the gemstone. They are known for their friendly and outgoing personalities, and make great pets for rat enthusiasts.

Citrine Rats:

Citrine rats have a coat that is a yellow-orange color, similar to the gemstone. They are known for their curious and energetic personalities, and make great pets for both children and adults.

Diamond Rats:

Diamond rats have a coat that is mostly white with black eyes. They are known for their friendly and social personalities, and make great pets for families with children.

Fluorite Rats:

Fluorite rats have a coat that is a purple or green color, similar to the gemstone. They are known for their calm and gentle personalities, and make great pets for rat enthusiasts.

Jade Rats:

Jade rats have a coat that is a light green color, similar to the gemstone. They are known for their curious and friendly personalities, and make great pets for both children and adults.

Lapis Rats:

Lapis rats have a coat that is a deep blue color, similar to the gemstone. They are known for their active and energetic personalities, and make great pets for rat enthusiasts.

Moonstone Rats:

Moonstone rats have a coat that is a white or gray color with a slight blue tint. They are known for their gentle and docile personalities, and make great pets for families with children.

Obsidian Rats:

Obsidian rats have a coat that is mostly black with some white hairs mixed in. They are known for their friendly and social personalities, and make great pets for rat enthusiasts.

Onyx Rats:

Onyx rats have a coat that is a shiny black color, similar to the gemstone. They are known for their active and playful personalities, and make great pets for both children and adults.

Quartz Rats:

Quartz rats have a coat that is a clear or white color, similar to the gemstone. They are known for their curious and friendly personalities, and make great pets for rat enthusiasts.

Turquoise Rats:

Turquoise rats have a coat that is a blue-green color, similar to the gemstone. They are known for their calm and gentle personalities, and make great pets for families with children.

Zircon Rats:

Zircon rats have a coat that is a blue or red color, similar to the gemstone. They are known for their playful and social personalities.

Grey rats:

Grey rats, also known as blue rats, have a coat that is a uniform grey or blue-grey color. They are a popular color in the rat fancy and are known for their docile and friendly temperament. Grey rats can also come in different shades, such as dark grey or light grey.

Brown rats:

Brown rats, also known as agouti rats, have a coat that is a mixture of brown and black with a white underbelly. They are one of the most common types of domesticated rats and are known for their inquisitive and social nature. Brown rats can also have different shades of brown, such as chocolate or cinnamon.

Black rats:

Black rats have a uniform black coat with a white underbelly. They are one of the original colors in the rat fancy and are known for their curious and active nature. Black rats can also come in different shades, such as a dark black or a softer grey-black.

Please note that this is not an exhaustive list, and there may be other breeds and variations of domesticated rats that are not listed here.

# 5. One or more

Deciding on the number of rats to own is an important consideration when it comes to pet rat ownership. While some rat owners opt for a single rat, others choose to keep multiple rats. There are pros and cons to both approaches, and it ultimately comes down to personal preference and circumstance.

One Rat:

Pros:

Easier to Bond:

With only one rat, it may be easier to establish a strong bond with your pet. This is because you can devote more attention to a single rat, and the rat may come to rely on you more as their sole companion.

Lower Maintenance

Costs: Owning one rat means you only need to provide for the needs of one rat, which can reduce the overall cost of food, bedding, and veterinary care.

Easier to Manage:

One rat is much easier to manage than multiple rats. You won't have to worry about introducing new rats or managing conflicts between rats.

Cons:

Loneliness:

Rats are social creatures and thrive on companionship. With only one rat, your pet may become lonely, leading to stress and depression.

Need for Human Interaction:

With no other rats to interact with, your rat may become overly reliant on human interaction for socialization, which can lead to boredom and frustration.

Lack of Enrichment:

With only one rat, you may find it challenging to provide enough stimulation and enrichment to keep your pet happy and engaged.

Multiple Rats:

Pros:

Socialization:

With multiple rats, you are providing your pets with the opportunity to engage in natural social behaviors. This can lead to happier, healthier, and more well-adjusted pets.

Less Lonely:

Multiple rats can keep each other company, reducing the chances of loneliness and depression in your pets.

Increased Enrichment:

With multiple rats, you can provide more stimulation and enrichment through toys, tunnels, and other accessories.

Cons:

More Maintenance:

Owning multiple rats means you'll need to provide for the needs of each rat, which can increase the overall cost of food, bedding, and veterinary care.

Greater Risk of Illness:

With more rats in close proximity, there is a greater risk of illness spreading throughout the group.

Potential for Conflict:

Multiple rats can lead to conflicts within the group, which can be difficult to manage and may require separating rats.

Deciding whether to own one rat or multiple rats is a personal decision that depends on your lifestyle, budget, and personal preferences. While both approaches have their pros and cons, it's essential to ensure that you can provide for the needs of each rat and offer a happy, healthy environment for your pets.

## 6. Cost of owning a Rat

Rats are a popular choice for pets due to their intelligence, playfulness, and affectionate nature. However, owning a rat comes with certain costs that must be considered before bringing one into your home. The cost of owning a rat can vary depending on several factors, including the rat's breed, age, and health, as well as the owner's location and lifestyle.

Initial Costs:

The initial cost of owning a rat includes the purchase price of the rat, the cage, bedding, food, water bottle, and toys. The cost of a rat can range from $5 to $40, depending on the breed and location. A good quality cage suitable for a rat can cost anywhere from $50 to $200, while bedding, food, and toys can cost up to $50 or more.

Ongoing Costs:

The ongoing cost of owning a rat includes food, bedding, toys, and medical expenses. The cost of food for a rat can range from $5 to $20 per month, while bedding and toys can cost up to $10 per month. Medical expenses for a rat can include routine checkups, vaccinations, and treatments for illnesses or injuries. The cost of veterinary care can vary, but it is important to have a budget of at least $100 to $200 per year for routine care.

Unexpected Costs:

Unexpected costs can arise when owning a rat, including emergency medical expenses, unexpected cage repairs or replacements, and other unforeseen expenses. It is important to have a savings account for these unexpected costs, which can range from $100 to $500 or more.

Time and Effort:

Owning a rat also requires time and effort. Rats require daily attention, including feeding, cleaning, and socialization. It is important to factor in the time and effort required to care for a rat when considering the cost of ownership.

Cost-Saving Tips:

There are several ways to save money when owning a rat, including buying food and bedding in bulk, making homemade toys, and finding low-cost veterinary clinics or pet insurance. It is also important to keep the rat's cage clean and well-maintained to prevent illnesses or injuries, which can result in costly medical bills.

Owning a rat comes with certain costs that must be considered before bringing one into your home. The initial cost of owning a rat includes the purchase price of the rat and the cage, while ongoing costs include food, bedding, toys, and medical expenses. Unexpected costs can arise, and it is important to have a savings account for these unexpected expenses. Owning a rat also requires time and effort, and there are ways to save money, such as buying in bulk and finding low-cost veterinary clinics or pet insurance. By considering these costs and cost-saving tips, owning a rat can be a rewarding and affordable experience.

These prices may be inaccurate in the future so it is best to do your own research before buying your pet rat.

## 7. Children and Rats

Rats can make wonderful pets for children, but it is important to ensure that both the children and the rats are properly supervised to prevent any accidents or injuries.

First, it is important to teach children how to properly handle and interact with rats. Children should be taught to approach rats calmly and gently, and to avoid sudden movements or loud noises that may startle or frighten the rats. It is also important to teach children to never pick up a rat by its tail, as this can cause serious harm to the rat.

It is also important to supervise children when they are interacting with rats to prevent any accidental injuries. Children should be reminded to wash their hands before and after handling the rats to prevent the spread of germs and disease.

When introducing rats to children, it is important to start slowly and allow the rats to get used to the new environment and people. It is also important to give the rats plenty of space and hiding places, as well as toys and activities to keep them occupied and entertained.

Children should also be taught to respect the rats' boundaries and to never force them to do anything they are uncomfortable with. This includes not picking up rats that do not want to be picked up, and allowing rats to come to them on their own terms.

Overall, rats can be wonderful pets for children, but it is important to ensure that both the children and the rats are properly supervised and that the children are taught how to properly handle and interact with the rats.

## 8. Rats and Other Pets

If you're already a pet owner, you may wonder how your rats will get along with your other pets. While rats are social and generally friendly, it's important to take certain precautions when introducing them to other animals.

Dogs:

Introducing rats to dogs can be tricky. Some dogs have a strong prey drive and may see rats as something to chase and attack. It's important to never leave rats unsupervised with dogs, especially in the early stages of their introduction. Start by keeping the rat in a cage and let your dog get used to their presence without direct interaction. Gradually let the rat out under supervision, and use positive reinforcement to reward your dog for calm behavior around the rat. With time, many dogs can learn to coexist peacefully with rats.

Cats:

Cats are natural predators and may view rats as prey. Similarly to introducing rats to dogs, it's important to never leave them unsupervised together. Start by keeping the rat in a secure cage, and allow your cat to observe from a distance. Use positive reinforcement to reward your cat for calm behavior around the rat. Gradually allow the rat out of their cage while still keeping a close eye on interactions.

Other small pets:

Rats can generally get along well with other small pets such as hamsters, gerbils, and mice. However, it's important to never house different species of small animals together, as they may fight and injure each other. It's also important to be aware of any potential diseases that can be transmitted between different species of small animals.

Birds:

It's not recommended to house rats and birds together, as rats may pose a threat to the bird's safety. Rats are known to be able to climb and may be able to reach the bird's cage, and even if the bird is outside of the cage, a rat may be tempted to chase and attack it.

Reptiles:

It's generally not recommended to house rats and reptiles together. While some species of reptiles are harmless, others may see rats as prey and may attack them. Additionally, rats may be able to access and damage the reptile's enclosure.

In conclusion, it's important to take careful steps when introducing rats to other pets. Always supervise interactions and never leave different species of animals unsupervised together. With time and patience, many pets can learn to coexist peacefully with rats.

## 9. Preparing your home

Preparing your home for rats is an essential step in providing a safe and comfortable environment for your new pets. Here are some tips to help you get your home ready:

Choose the right location:

Select a room or area in your home that is free from drafts, has good ventilation, and is away from direct sunlight, loud noises, and other pets.

Set up the cage:

Choose a cage that is large enough to accommodate your rats comfortably, with enough room for them to move around, play, and exercise. The cage should be made of sturdy materials, with a solid floor, and easy to clean. Make sure the cage has enough bedding and nesting material for your rats to feel cozy and secure.

Provide food and water:

Provide your rats with a balanced diet, consisting of a high-quality commercial rat food, fresh fruits, vegetables, and treats. Rats need access to fresh, clean water at all times, so make sure to provide a water bottle or dish that is easy for them to access.

Rat-proof your home:

Rats are curious and love to explore, so it's important to rat-proof your home to prevent accidents and keep them safe. Cover any holes, gaps, or openings where rats could escape or get trapped. Keep household chemicals, plants, and other potential hazards out of reach.

Create a play area:

Rats are active and social animals that need plenty of opportunities to play and interact with their environment. Set up a play area in your home, with toys, tunnels, and climbing structures that your rats can enjoy.

Plan for vet visits:

Rats need regular check-ups and preventative care, just like any other pet. Make sure to find a veterinarian who is experienced in treating rats and budget for regular vet visits and any unexpected medical expenses.

By following these tips, you can create a safe and enjoyable environment for your rats to thrive in. Remember, rats are intelligent and social animals that require daily interaction, play, and attention from their owners. With the right care and preparation, owning rats can be a rewarding and fulfilling experience.

# 10. Enclosure

When it comes to cage style, there are a few options to choose from. Wire cages are the most popular type of cage for rats. They provide good ventilation, are easy to clean and allow for plenty of climbing opportunities. However, wire floors can be hard on rat's feet, so it's important to choose a cage with a solid floor or use a layer of bedding to cover the wire floor.

Another option is a glass or plastic tank. These cages provide a secure environment and are easy to clean, but they can be heavy and are not as well-ventilated as wire cages. Here are some things to consider when choosing a cage for your rat:

Size:

Rats are active and intelligent animals that require a lot of space to run and play. The cage should be big enough to accommodate your rat and its accessories, including a litter box, food and water dishes, and toys. A good rule of thumb is that the cage should be at least 2 cubic feet of space per rat

Bar spacing:

The spacing between the bars should be no more than 1 inch to prevent your rat from escaping or getting its head stuck between the bars.

Material:

The cage should be made of sturdy and non-toxic materials. Avoid cages made of plastic or thin wire, as rats can easily chew through them. A cage made of coated wire or powder-coated metal is a good option.

Accessibility:

Make sure the cage has easy access for cleaning and maintenance. A removable tray at the bottom of the cage is ideal for easy cleaning.

Multi-level:

Rats love to climb and explore, so a multi-level cage with ramps and platforms is a great option. This will provide your rat with plenty of opportunities for exercise and mental stimulation.

Location:

The cage should be located in a quiet and peaceful area of your home, away from direct sunlight, drafts, and other pets. Rats are social animals, so placing the cage in a busy area of the house where they can interact with their human family is a good idea.

Bedding:

Avoid using cedar or pine bedding, as the strong scent can irritate your rat's respiratory system. Also, be sure to clean your rat's cage regularly to keep it smelling fresh and to prevent the buildup of bacteria.

For bedding, rats need a comfortable and absorbent material to sleep on and to absorb their urine and feces. Avoid cedar and pine shavings, as they can cause respiratory problems. Instead, choose bedding made from paper, aspen shavings, or a paper-based pellet bedding. These types of bedding are safe and easy to clean.

To keep your rat's cage clean and fresh, you will need to provide a litter box. A litter box can be filled with the same type of bedding used throughout the cage, and should be cleaned and refreshed daily.

Rats also need a place to hide and nest. A cozy hideaway, such as a small igloo or a cardboard box, will provide your rat with a secure place to rest and feel safe.

## 11. Bedding

Choosing the right bedding for your pet rat is essential for their health and comfort. Rats spend a lot of time in their cages, so it is important to choose bedding that is safe and appropriate for their needs.

The first consideration when choosing bedding is safety. Avoid cedar and pine shavings, as they can cause respiratory problems and other health issues for rats. These types of wood contain volatile oils that can irritate the respiratory system and lead to respiratory infections. Additionally, cedar and pine shavings can contain phenols, which are toxic to rats and other small animals.

Instead of cedar and pine shavings, opt for bedding made from paper, aspen shavings, or a paper-based pellet bedding. These types of bedding are safe and easy to clean. Paper-based bedding is a popular choice because it is absorbent, dust-free, and environmentally friendly. Aspen shavings are also a good option because they are absorbent and odor-controlling.

Another factor to consider when choosing bedding is absorbency. Rats produce a lot of urine, so it is important to choose bedding that can absorb moisture effectively. Paper-based bedding and aspen shavings are both good options for absorbency.

Another consideration is dust. Some types of bedding can produce dust, which can irritate your rat's respiratory system. Paper-based bedding and aspen shavings are both relatively dust-free, making them good choices for rats.

When choosing bedding, you will also need to consider your budget. Paper-based bedding can be more expensive than aspen shavings or other types of bedding, so it may not be the best choice if you are on a tight budget. However, paper-based bedding is generally considered the safest and most comfortable option for rats.

In addition to the type of bedding, you will also need to consider the thickness of the bedding. Rats like to burrow and nest, so providing them with enough bedding to do so is important. A layer of bedding that is at least 2-3 inches thick is recommended.

Lastly, consider the ease of cleaning when choosing bedding. Paper-based bedding and aspen shavings are both easy to clean and maintain, making them popular choices for rat owners.

## 12. Toys and Accessories

Toys are an essential part of a rat's life as they provide mental and physical stimulation, and help prevent boredom and stress. There are many types of toys available for rats, and it is important to choose toys that are safe, durable, and appropriate for your rat's age and size.

Climbing toys:

Climbing toys, such as ropes, ladders, and branches. Rats are natural climbers and enjoy exploring their environment, so providing climbing opportunities can help keep them physically active and mentally stimulated. It is important to make sure the climbing toys are securely attached and are made of non-toxic materials.

Tunnels and Hideouts:

Rats enjoy having a place to hide and feel secure, so providing a tunnel or small house can give them a sense of security and privacy. Tunnels and hideouts can be made of various materials, such as cardboard, PVC pipe, or wood. However, it is important to make sure the materials are safe for your rat to chew on and are not toxic.

Chew toys:

are also important for rats as they help keep their teeth healthy and prevent them from becoming overgrown. Rats have teeth that grow continuously, and they need to chew on hard objects to wear down their teeth. Chew toys can be made of wood, mineral blocks, or hard plastic. It is important to choose chew toys that are safe and durable and do not have small parts that can be swallowed.

Interactive toys:

Puzzle feeders and treat balls, can also provide mental stimulation for rats. These types of toys require the rat to use their problem-solving skills to access the food or treats inside, which can help keep their minds active and engaged.

When choosing toys for your rat, it is important to consider their safety and durability. Toys should be made of non-toxic materials, and any loose parts should be securely attached. It is also important to rotate toys regularly to prevent boredom and to keep your rat interested and engaged. Finally, it is important to monitor your rat when they are playing with toys to ensure their safety and prevent any injuries.

These items can be purchased at a pet store, or you can make your own toys at home.

Accessories:

Along with toys, there are several other accessories that are important for your rat's health and happiness. Here are some common accessories you may want to consider for your rat:

Hammocks:

Rats love to climb and explore, and hammocks provide a great place for them to rest and relax.

Litter boxes:

Rats can be litter trained, which makes cleaning their cage easier. A small litter box with paper or wood pellets can be placed in one corner of the cage to encourage your rat to use it.

Wheels:

Exercise wheels can provide a great outlet for your rat's energy. Make sure to choose a wheel that is appropriately sized for your rat to prevent injury.

Chews:

Rats have constantly growing teeth and need to chew to keep them healthy. Chews made from wood or hard plastic can help keep their teeth in good condition.

Water bottles:

Water bottles are a better option than bowls as they keep the water clean and prevent spills. Be sure to choose a bottle that is appropriate for your rat's size.

Food dishes:

A sturdy, heavy dish is ideal for feeding your rat. Avoid dishes made of plastic or other chewable materials, as rats may chew on them and ingest small pieces.

## 13. Choosing a rat

Choosing a rat can be an exciting and rewarding experience, but it's important to consider several factors before bringing one home. Here are some things to keep in mind when choosing a rat.

Gender:

When deciding to bring home a rat as a pet, one of the first decisions you will need to make is whether to choose a male or female rat. Both male and female rats make great pets, but there are some differences between the genders that you should consider before making your choice.

Male rats tend to be larger and more muscular than females, and they are typically more active and playful. They may also be more social and enjoy interacting with their owners. However, male rats have a strong odor that can be unpleasant for some people. This odor is caused by their hormones, and it can be reduced by neutering.

Female rats are generally smaller than males and tend to be more docile and gentle. They may be less active and playful than males, but they are also less likely to fight with other rats. Female rats do not have the strong odor that male rats do, but they may experience hormonal fluctuations that can lead to mood swings and aggression. Spaying can help prevent these hormonal changes.

It is important to note that both male and female rats can be trained and socialized, so the decision ultimately comes down to personal preference. If you want a more active and playful pet, a male rat may be a better choice for you. If you prefer a more docile and gentle pet, a female rat may be a better fit. It is also important to consider the potential health issues that can arise with each gender, such as mammary tumors in females and testicular tumors in males.

Age:

Rats can live for up to 3 years, so it's important to choose one that is healthy and young. Younger rats are generally easier to train and socialize, and they also tend to be more active and playful.

Health:

When choosing a rat, make sure to choose one that is healthy and free of any visible health problems. Look for rats that have bright, clear eyes, a shiny coat, and are alert and active. Avoid rats that show any signs of lethargy, discharge from the eyes or nose, or any other signs of illness.

Personality:

Each rat has its own unique personality, so it's important to spend some time with the rat before bringing it home. Look for rats that are friendly, curious, and playful. Avoid rats that are timid, aggressive, or show any signs of anxiety or stress.

Breeder or Pet Store:

When deciding where to acquire a new rat, you may have the option of getting one from a breeder or a pet store. Both options have their pros and cons, so it is important to consider your priorities before making a decision.

Breeder:

Pros:

Breeders generally have a greater knowledge and expertise of the rats they breed, their personalities, and their genetic history.

You may have the option of choosing a specific breed or lineage of rat.

Breeders are typically more invested in their rats and may provide more information and support after you bring your rat home.

Cons:

Rats from a breeder are usually more expensive than those from a pet store.

Breeders may not always have rats available when you are looking to get one.

You may have to travel further to get your rat from a breeder.

Pet Store:

Pros:

Pet stores are usually more accessible than breeders and may have rats available at any time.

Rats from pet stores are generally less expensive than those from breeders.

Pet stores may offer discounts or promotions on rat supplies when you purchase a rat from them.

Cons:

Pet stores may not have the same level of knowledge or expertise on the rats they sell as breeders do.

The rats may have been bred for quantity rather than quality, which can result in health or behavioral issues.

There is a risk of supporting unethical breeding practices if the pet store sources rats from a supplier that engages in mass breeding or inhumane conditions.

In either case, it is important to research the breeder or pet store beforehand to ensure they have a good reputation and take proper care of their rats.

Rat's Appearance:

Rats come in many different colors and patterns, so you'll want to choose one that appeals to you. Keep in mind that while the rat's appearance is important, it should not be the only factor you consider when choosing a rat.

Overall, when choosing a rat, it's important to take your time, do your research, and consider all of the factors involved. By choosing a healthy, friendly, and well-adjusted rat, you'll be well on your way to building a long and rewarding relationship with your new pet.

## 14. Bringing home

Bringing home a new pet rat can be an exciting and rewarding experience, but it's important to be prepared for the first few days. Here's what you can expect during this time:

Adjustment Period:

It's normal for rats to take some time to adjust to their new surroundings. During the first few days, your rat may seem nervous or shy. Give them plenty of time to explore their new environment at their own pace. Avoid making sudden movements or loud noises that may startle them.

Appetite Changes:

Your rat's appetite may change during the first few days. They may not eat as much as they did before or may not eat at all. This is normal and may be due to stress from the move. Offer them their favorite foods and treats and make sure fresh water is available at all times.

Socialization:

Rats are social animals and need plenty of interaction with their owners. Spend time with your rat every day, talking to them, and offering them treats. Be gentle and patient, and your rat will start to trust you.

Litter Training:

If you plan to keep your rat in a cage, it's important to litter train them. Place a litter box in their cage and encourage them to use it. If your rat has accidents outside of the litter box, gently place them back in the box and offer a treat as a reward when they use it correctly.

Health Concerns:

During the first few days, keep an eye on your rat's health. Look for signs of illness such as runny nose, discharge from the eyes, or lethargy. If you notice anything concerning, contact your veterinarian immediately.

By being patient and gentle with your new pet rat, you can help them adjust to their new home and form a strong bond with you. Remember to provide them with plenty of love, attention, and a safe and comfortable living environment.

## 15. Bring another Rat home

Introducing a new rat to your existing rat or rats can be a delicate process that requires patience and careful planning. It is important to take the necessary steps to ensure a smooth introduction, as this can help prevent fighting and establish a harmonious living situation for all rats involved.

The first step is to make sure that the new rat is healthy and has been quarantined for at least two weeks to ensure that they are not carrying any diseases that could be passed on to your existing rats. Once the new rat has been cleared, it's time to start the introduction process.

The first introduction should be done in a neutral territory, such as a bathtub or a playpen, where neither rat has established dominance or territorial boundaries. Provide plenty of toys and hideaways to encourage exploration and provide a safe place for each rat to retreat to if necessary.

During the first introduction, it is important to closely monitor the rats for any signs of aggression. This includes puffing up, hair standing on end, and lunging. If any aggression is observed, separate the rats immediately and try again at a later time.

Assuming the first introduction goes well, it is time to move on to the next step, which is to allow short, supervised visits between the rats in the existing rat's home territory. This will allow the rats to get used to each other's scent and establish a hierarchy.

During this stage, it is important to provide plenty of resources, such as food and water dishes, toys, and hiding spots, to prevent competition and reduce the chances of fighting.

Over time, you can gradually increase the length and frequency of these supervised visits until the rats are comfortable together and can be left alone without any fighting.

It is important to note that some rats may never fully accept a new rat and may require permanent separation. However, with patience and careful management, most rats can be successfully integrated into a group.

# 16. Bonding

Bonding with your pet rat or rats is an essential part of building a trusting and loving relationship. This process can take time, but with patience and consistent effort, you can form a strong and meaningful bond with your rat.

When you first bring your rat home, it is important to give them time to adjust to their new environment. Allow them to explore their new cage and surroundings at their own pace. Resist the urge to handle them right away, as they may feel scared and stressed.

Instead spend some time sitting quietly near the cage and speaking softly to your rat. You can offer your rat/rats a treat through the bars of the cage to help them feel more comfortable with you.

Next offering treats through the cage bars, allowing your rat to approach and take them from your hand. This will help them associate you with positive experiences.

Once your rat is comfortable taking treats from your hand, you can begin to handle them. Start by placing your hand in the cage and allowing your rat to climb onto it. Be sure to support their body and move slowly and gently. Gradually increase the amount of time you spend holding your rat, and offer treats and praise to reinforce positive behavior.

As your rat becomes more comfortable with you, spend more time interacting with them outside of the cage. Playtime is a great way to bond with your rat and help them get the exercise and mental stimulation they need. Toys and accessories can also be used during playtime to help your rat feel more comfortable and to encourage interaction.

As your bond with your rat grows stronger, you can begin to work on training and teaching your rat new skills and tricks. Positive reinforcement training is an effective and rewarding way to train your rat and to strengthen your bond with them. You can use treats and praise to reward your rat for good behavior and to reinforce positive interactions.

It is important to spend time with your rat every day, offering them attention and affection. Gently stroke their back or head, or play with them using toys or treats. This will help them associate you with positive experiences and build trust.

In addition to handling and playtime, it is important to provide your rat with a consistent routine. Offer food and water at the same time every day, and keep their cage clean and comfortable. Rats thrive on routine and will feel more secure and happy when they know what to expect.

As your rat matures and grows, continue to spend time with them every day, providing affection and attention. Remember to respect your rat's boundaries and preferences, and allow them to approach you on their own terms. With patience and love, you can form a deep and meaningful bond with your pet rat.

## 17. Feeding your Rat

Feeding your rat a balanced and nutritious diet is essential for its health and well-being. Rats are omnivores, which means they eat both plant and animal-based foods. A healthy diet for a pet rat should include a variety of fresh fruits, vegetables, grains, and protein sources. In this chapter, we will discuss the best foods to feed your pet rat, how much to feed, and how to prevent overfeeding.

Best Foods for Rats

Vegetables:

Kale

Spinach

Collard greens

Dark leafy greens are particularly important, as they are high in vitamin A, calcium, and iron

Other vegetables:

Carrots

Bell peppers

Zucchini

Broccoli

These vegetables are high in fiber and other important nutrients that can help keep your rat healthy.

Treat vegetables:

Sweet potatoes

Peas

Corn

These vegetables are higher in sugar and should only be given occasionally in moderation.

When introducing new vegetables to your rat's diet, it is important to do so gradually to avoid digestive upset. Start with a small amount and gradually increase over time.

Remember to always wash vegetables thoroughly before feeding them to your rat to remove any pesticides or other contaminants. Additionally, avoid feeding your rat any vegetables that are **toxic to rats, such as onion, garlic, and avocado.**

Fruits:

Apples, remove the seeds and core before feeding.

Bananas, peel and cut into small pieces.

Blueberries, wash thoroughly before feeding.

Grapes, remove the seeds before feeding.

Melons, remove the seeds and rind before feeding.

Treat fruits:

Raisins

Cranberries

Apricots

However, be sure to limit the amount of dried fruits as they are high in sugar and can lead to weight gain and dental issues if overfed. It is also important to **avoid sugary fruits such as cherries and figs, as well as citrus fruits**, which can upset your rat's digestive system.

Fruits are a great addition to a rat's diet as they provide essential vitamins and minerals. However, due to their high sugar content, they should only be fed in moderation. A good rule of thumb is to offer about 1-2 teaspoons of fruit per rat per day.

Protein Sources:

Cooked chicken, is another excellent source of protein for rats. You can cook the chicken in various ways, such as boiled or baked, and offer it to your rats in small amounts.

Tofu, is a great source of protein for rats that are on a vegetarian diet. It is low in fat and can be served raw or cooked.

Fish, can be a good source of protein. Make sure the fish is cooked and deboned before offering it to your rats.

High-quality commercial rat food, this is the main source of protein for most pet rats. Look for a high-quality commercial food that is specifically formulated for rats and contains at least 16% protein.

Treat Protein:

Hard-boiled eggs , should be given in moderation as they are high in cholesterol.

It is important to note that while these protein sources are safe for rats, they should be given in moderation as part of a balanced diet. Too much protein can lead to health problems.

Grains and Seeds:

1-2 almonds

1-2 walnuts

1-2 pecans

1-2 hazelnuts

1-2 pumpkin seeds

1-2 sunflower seeds

Treat Nuts and Seeds:

Peanut butter (in small amounts)

Unsalted popcorn

Unsalted nuts and seeds (in moderation)

Dried fruits (in moderation)

**It's important to note that some nuts and seeds, such as macadamia nuts and avocado pits, are toxic to rats and should be avoided.**

When giving your rat nuts and seeds as a treat, be sure to limit their intake and choose unsalted varieties. Also, avoid giving your rat sweetened or flavored nuts or seeds as they may contain harmful additives.

Cooked pasta, rice, and oats:

Can be a good addition to a rat's diet, but they should be given in moderation as they are high in carbohydrates. A small amount of cooked pasta, rice, or oats can be given to rats once or twice a week as a treat.

When feeding cooked pasta, rice, or oats to rats, it is important to make sure that the food is fully cooked and cooled before giving it to them. Any leftovers should be refrigerated and used within a few days.

A good rule of thumb for portion size is to give your rat a piece of cooked pasta or a spoonful of cooked rice or oats that is about the size of their head. It is better to start with a smaller amount and increase gradually if necessary, as overfeeding can lead to obesity and other health problems.

Overall, cooked pasta, rice, and oats can be a tasty addition to a rat's diet, but they should be given in moderation and as a treat rather than a regular part of their daily meals.

Cheese:

Can be a tasty treat for rats, but it should be fed in moderation as it is high in fat and salt. It is not recommended to make cheese a regular part of a rat's diet, but rather an occasional treat.

The amount of cheese that is safe to feed a rat depends on their age, weight, and overall health. As a general rule, a small piece of cheese about the size of a pea or a thumbnail can be given as a treat once or twice a week.

Yogurt:

Can be a healthy addition to a rat's diet in moderation. It is a good source of protein and calcium, which are important for maintaining healthy bones and muscles.

When giving yogurt to your rats, choose plain, unsweetened yogurt without any added flavors or sweeteners. Avoid yogurt that contains artificial sweeteners or high levels of sugar. Greek yogurt is a good option as it is high in protein.

Start by giving your rats a small amount of yogurt as a treat, such as a tablespoon or less. Observe how they react to it and ensure that they are able to tolerate it well. If they have any signs of gastrointestinal upset such as diarrhea, reduce or eliminate the amount of yogurt given. Like cheese this should only be given once or twice a week.

It is important to note that some rats may have trouble digesting dairy products, including cheese and yogurt. Signs of lactose intolerance in rats can include diarrhea, bloating, and gas. If your rat shows any of these symptoms after eating cheese, it may be best to avoid feeding it to them in the future.

Water:

It is important to provide your rat with fresh, clean water at all times. You can use a water bottle or a small dish for water, and make sure to change it daily.

How Much to Feed Your Rat?

The amount of food you should feed your rat depends on its age, weight, and activity level. Adult rats typically need 15-20 grams of food per day, while younger rats may need more. You can divide their food into two or three meals a day. Monitor your rat's weight regularly to ensure it is maintaining a healthy weight.

Preventing Overfeeding.

Rats have a tendency to overeat, which can lead to obesity and other health problems. To prevent overfeeding, measure out your rat's food portions and avoid giving your rat unlimited access to food. It is also important to limit treats, as they can be high in sugar and calories.

A well-balanced diet is crucial for the health and well-being of your pet rat. A balanced diet should include a variety of foods, including fruits, vegetables, animal proteins, and others. Here is a breakdown of the recommended percentage of each type of food in a rat's diet:

Fruits: 10-15%

Fruits should be given to rats in moderation due to their high sugar content. Good options include apples, bananas, berries, melons, and pears.

Vegetables: 20-25%

Vegetables should make up a significant portion of your rat's diet. Good options include leafy greens (spinach, kale, lettuce), broccoli, carrots, peas, sweet potatoes, and squash.

Animal proteins: 15-20%

Rats are omnivores and require animal proteins in their diet. Good options include cooked chicken, turkey, beef, eggs, and fish.

Seeds, nuts, and grains: 5-10%

Seeds, nuts, and grains should be given in moderation as they are high in fat. Good options include sunflower seeds, pumpkin seeds, flaxseed, oats, quinoa, and brown rice.

Other foods: 30-40%

This category includes treats and other foods that can be given to rats in moderation. Good options include yogurt, cheese, cooked pasta, and bread.

It is important to note that these percentages can vary based on individual rat needs and preferences. Always monitor your rat's weight and adjust their diet as needed.

## 18. Cleaning the Rat's Cage

Rats are social and active creatures that require a clean and comfortable living environment to thrive. As a responsible pet owner, it's important to keep your rat's cage clean and hygienic to prevent the build-up of bacteria, odors, and health issues. In this chapter, we'll discuss the importance of cleaning your rat's cage, how often to clean it, and the proper steps to do so.

Why Cleaning the Rat's Cage is Important

Keeping your rat's cage clean is important for several reasons. Firstly, rats are susceptible to respiratory infections and other illnesses caused by poor hygiene. A dirty cage can harbor bacteria, viruses, and parasites that can affect your rat's health. Secondly, rats are naturally curious and love to explore their surroundings. They may try to eat anything they find in their cage, including their own feces or urine, which can also lead to health problems.

How Often Should You Clean the Rat's Cage?

The frequency of cleaning your rat's cage depends on several factors, such as the size of the cage, the number of rats you have, and the type of bedding you use. In general, it's recommended to do a full cleaning of the cage once a week, along with spot cleaning as needed throughout the week.

Spot cleaning involves removing any visible droppings, food debris, or soiled bedding daily. This helps maintain a cleaner environment for your rat and prevents the accumulation of harmful bacteria and odors. A full cleaning of the cage involves removing all the bedding, toys, and accessories from the cage, cleaning them thoroughly, and disinfecting the cage itself.

Steps to Cleaning the Rat's Cage:

Prepare a safe and secure area for your rat:

Before starting the cleaning process, make sure your rat has a safe and secure area to stay in while you clean their cage.

Remove all items from the cage:

Take out all the bedding, toys, and accessories from the cage and place them in a separate area.

Dispose of any disposable items:

If you use disposable bedding or litter, dispose of it in the appropriate manner.

Clean the cage:

Use a pet-safe disinfectant and warm water to clean the cage thoroughly. Make sure to scrub all surfaces, corners, and crevices of the cage. Rinse the cage with clean water and let it dry completely before placing new bedding inside.

Clean and disinfect accessories:

Clean and disinfect all toys, food bowls, and water bottles before putting them back in the cage.

Add fresh bedding:

Put fresh bedding inside the cage, making sure to provide enough depth for your rat to burrow and nest in.

Reassemble the cage:

Put all the accessories and toys back in the cage, making sure they're arranged in a way that allows your rat to move around and explore.

Cleaning your rat's cage is an essential part of owning a pet rat. By maintaining a clean and hygienic environment, you'll help keep your rat healthy and happy. Regular cleaning also helps prevent unpleasant odors and makes it easier to bond with your pet. With the right approach and tools, cleaning your rat's cage can be a simple and straightforward task.

## 19. Grooming

Grooming your rat is an essential aspect of their care that helps keep them healthy and happy. Rats are naturally clean animals and will groom themselves regularly. However, as a rat owner, it's your responsibility to ensure that your pet's grooming needs are met.

Brushing:

Is an important aspect of rat grooming, as it helps to distribute natural oils throughout the fur, removes loose fur and dirt, and prevents matting. Brushing your rat can also provide an opportunity for bonding and can help keep your rat calm and relaxed.

When brushing your rat, use a soft-bristled brush and gently stroke in the direction of the fur. Start at the head and work your way down the body, taking care around sensitive areas such as the face and tail. Brush your rat regularly, at least once a week, to keep their coat healthy and shiny.

Some rats may enjoy being brushed more than others, so it is important to start slowly and be patient. Offer treats and positive reinforcement to encourage your rat to stay still and calm during brushing sessions.

In addition to brushing, you can also use a damp cloth to wipe down your rat's fur and clean any areas that may become dirty or soiled. Avoid using soap or shampoo unless absolutely necessary, as rats are able to groom themselves and excessive bathing can strip the fur of natural oils.

Overall, regular brushing and gentle cleaning can help keep your rat healthy and happy, and can strengthen the bond between you and your pet.

Nail care:

Overgrown nails can cause discomfort and pain for your rat, and may even lead to injury or infection. Trimming your rat's nails on a regular basis can help prevent these issues and keep your pet healthy and happy.

Before you begin, make sure you have a pair of sharp, small animal nail clippers. It may also be helpful to have some styptic powder or cornstarch on hand in case you accidentally cut the quick, which can cause bleeding.

To trim your rat's nails, start by gently holding your rat in your lap or on a flat surface. Use one hand to hold the rat securely, and use the other hand to gently extend the paw you want to trim. Carefully inspect the nail to locate the quick, which is the pink portion of the nail that contains blood vessels and nerves. It is important to avoid cutting the quick, as this can cause bleeding and pain.

Once you have identified the quick, use the nail clippers to make a small, quick snip of the nail. It is better to make multiple small cuts rather than one large cut to avoid accidentally cutting the quick. If you do accidentally cut the quick, immediately apply styptic powder or cornstarch to stop the bleeding.

After you have trimmed all of your rat's nails, reward them with a treat or some extra attention to make the experience more positive. Repeat this process every 2-4 weeks, depending on the rate of nail growth.

Regular nail trimming is an important aspect of rat care and can help keep your pet comfortable and healthy.

Dental:

Maintaining good dental health is crucial for rats, as their teeth continually grow throughout their lives. It is important to provide rats with items to chew on to prevent their teeth from overgrowing, which can lead to painful dental problems.

One way to promote good dental health is by providing your rats with chew toys and items such as wooden blocks, untreated wooden sticks, and mineral blocks. These will help to wear down their teeth and keep them healthy.

It is also important to monitor your rat's teeth regularly to make sure they are not overgrowing or causing any discomfort. If you notice any problems with your rat's teeth, such as discoloration or abnormal growth, you should take them to the vet for an examination.

In some cases, your vet may recommend a dental cleaning or trimming to correct any dental issues. It is important to only have a qualified vet perform dental procedures on your rat, as they require specialized equipment and knowledge to do so safely.

In addition to providing chew toys and regular check-ups, you can also promote good dental health by feeding your rat a balanced and nutritious diet. This will help to prevent any nutritional deficiencies that can affect the health of their teeth and gums.

Maintaining good dental health is essential for the well-being of your pet rat. By providing appropriate chew toys, monitoring their teeth, and seeking veterinary care when needed, you can help keep your rat's teeth healthy and strong throughout their life.

Bathing:

Is not always necessary, as rats are generally clean animals and groom themselves regularly. However, there may be times when a bath is necessary, such as if your rat gets into something sticky or dirty.

Before bathing your rat, it's important to prepare a safe and comfortable environment. Choose a small plastic tub or sink that your rat can comfortably stand in, and fill it with warm water that is about 1-2 inches deep. You can add a few drops of a mild pet shampoo to the water if desired, but be sure to avoid getting any shampoo in your rat's eyes, ears, or nose.

To bathe your rat, gently place them into the water and use your hands to wet their fur thoroughly. Avoid getting water in their face, and use a washcloth or sponge to clean around their ears and face. Once your rat is wet, apply a small amount of shampoo and massage it into their fur, working from the head down to the tail.

Rinse your rat thoroughly with clean water, making sure to remove all traces of shampoo. Once your rat is clean, you can wrap them in a warm towel and gently dry them off. It's important to keep your rat warm and dry after a bath, as they can easily catch a chill.

It's important to note that frequent bathing can strip your rat's skin of natural oils and cause dryness and irritation. Therefore, it's best to limit baths to only when necessary. In between baths, you can use a soft brush or damp cloth to gently wipe down your rat's fur and keep them clean and comfortable.

Grooming your rat is a necessary part of their care that helps keep them healthy and happy. Regular brushing, nail trims, and dental checks are essential to maintain their well-being. Additionally, keeping their living space clean and well-maintained helps prevent illness and promotes good health.

# 20. Travelling

Plan ahead:

Before traveling with your rats, it's important to plan ahead to ensure that you have everything you need. This includes packing enough food, water, bedding, and any necessary medication for your rats. You should also research the rules and regulations for traveling with pets, especially if you're crossing state or national borders.

Choose a suitable carrier:

When traveling with rats, it's important to choose a carrier that is secure, well-ventilated, and appropriately sized for your rats. A good option is a small pet carrier with a solid bottom, secure latching mechanism, and air holes for ventilation.

Introduce the carrier to your rats:

If your rats are not used to being in a carrier, it's a good idea to introduce it to them before the trip. This can help them become more comfortable with the carrier and reduce stress during the trip.

Familiarize your rats with car rides:

Some rats may be prone to motion sickness, so it's a good idea to get them used to car rides before embarking on a long trip. You can start by taking them on short car rides and gradually increasing the duration.

Provide comfortable bedding:

It's important to provide your rats with comfortable bedding during the trip to help reduce stress. A good option is to line the carrier with shredded paper or paper-based bedding that your rats are familiar with.

Keep the carrier secure:

During the trip, it's important to keep the carrier secure to prevent it from sliding or tipping over. You can secure the carrier with a seatbelt or place it on a stable surface.

Offer food and water:

It's important to offer your rats food and water during the trip to prevent dehydration and hunger. You can offer water in a water bottle attached to the carrier and provide small portions of food in a separate container.

Take breaks:

If you're traveling a long distance, it's important to take breaks to allow your rats to stretch their legs, eat, drink, and use the bathroom. You can stop at a rest area or pet-friendly park for a break.

Monitor your rats:

It's important to monitor your rats during the trip to ensure that they are not showing signs of stress, illness, or injury. If you notice any unusual behavior, contact a veterinarian.

Provide a comfortable destination:

Once you reach your destination, it's important to provide your rats with a comfortable and familiar environment. This includes providing their regular food, water, and bedding, as well as any toys or accessories that they are used to.

## 20. Disease and symptoms

Domestic rats like all animals, they are susceptible to various diseases and health problems. Here are some of the most common illnesses and health issues that can affect pet rats:

Parasites:

Parasites can cause significant discomfort and health issues for rats, leading to skin irritations, hair loss, and excessive itching. Parasites are often transmitted through contact with other infected rats or through contact with contaminated bedding, food, or water.

One of the most common parasites that rats can acquire is lice. Lice are tiny insects that feed on the rat's blood and can cause intense itching, leading to hair loss and skin damage. These parasites can be transmitted through direct contact with infected rats, contaminated bedding, or other materials.

Mites are another type of parasite that can affect rats. These tiny arachnids can cause a condition known as mange, which can lead to hair loss, skin infections, and intense itching. Mites are often spread through contact with other infected rats or through contaminated bedding.

Fleas can also be a concern for rats, especially if they share living quarters with other animals such as dogs or cats. Fleas can cause skin irritations, hair loss, and other health problems in rats. They can be challenging to eliminate and often require treatment of the entire living environment, including bedding, furniture, and carpets.

It is essential to regularly check your rat for signs of parasites, including excessive scratching, hair loss, or visible insects on their fur. If you suspect your rat has parasites, seek veterinary care immediately to prevent further health complications. Regular cleaning and disinfection of the rat's living environment can also help prevent the spread of parasites.

Malocclusion:

Occurs when the teeth of a rat do not meet properly, leading to overgrowth, misalignment, and other dental issues. Malocclusion can be caused by genetics or poor nutrition, as well as injury or trauma to the teeth.

Symptoms of malocclusion include difficulty eating or drinking, weight loss, drooling, and jaw pain. Left untreated, malocclusion can cause a range of health problems, including dental infections, abscesses, and even death.

Megacolon:

A condition that affects the digestive system of rats, where the colon becomes enlarged and unable to contract properly, leading to constipation and other digestive issues. It can occur in rats of any age and is more common in male rats. Megacolon can be congenital or acquired and can be caused by various factors such as diet, genetics, and infection. The symptoms of megacolon include difficulty defecating, abdominal pain, loss of appetite, and lethargy. Treatment for megacolon may involve dietary changes, medication to help soften stool, and surgery in severe cases. It is important to monitor the diet and bowel movements of rats regularly to prevent and identify megacolon early.

Scurvy:

A condition that results from a deficiency in vitamin C, which is an essential nutrient for rats. Rats, unlike humans, cannot synthesize vitamin C on their own and therefore rely on dietary sources to meet their requirements. If a rat's diet is lacking in vitamin C, scurvy can occur, causing a range of symptoms. These symptoms may include lethargy, weakness, swollen or painful joints, difficulty breathing, and even death if left untreated.

Scurvy is a preventable condition and can be managed with appropriate dietary changes and supplementation. A balanced diet that includes adequate amounts of fresh fruits and vegetables that are high in vitamin C, such as oranges, kiwis, bell peppers, and broccoli, can help prevent scurvy. Vitamin C supplements can also be added to a rat's diet to ensure that they are meeting their daily requirements.

If you suspect that your rat may be suffering from scurvy, it is important to seek veterinary care. Your vet may recommend dietary changes and vitamin C supplementation, as well as other supportive care to manage your rat's symptoms. With proper treatment and management, most rats can recover from scurvy and go on to live healthy, happy lives.

Abscesses:

Can be caused by bacteria, such as Staphylococcus aureus. These pus-filled pockets can develop anywhere on the rat's body, but are most commonly found on the face, neck, and feet. They can be caused by a variety of factors, including injuries, bites, or scratches from other rats, or poor hygiene.

If left untreated, abscesses can cause serious health problems for rats, as they can spread and cause systemic infections. Signs that a rat may have an abscess include swelling, redness, warmth, and pain in the affected area. Rats may also display signs of discomfort, such as scratching or biting at the affected area.

Treatment for abscesses typically involves draining the pus and administering antibiotics to treat the infection. In severe cases, surgery may be necessary to remove the abscess. It is important to seek veterinary care as soon as possible if you suspect that your rat has an abscess, as prompt treatment can help prevent further complications. Additionally, practicing good hygiene and providing a clean living environment can help prevent abscesses from developing in the first place.

## Respiratory infections

Rats have very sensitive respiratory systems, and can be easily affected by airborne irritants and bacteria. They are particularly prone to respiratory infections when they are kept in damp or dirty environments.

The symptoms of respiratory infections in rats are similar to those in humans, and include sneezing, coughing, wheezing, and difficulty breathing. If left untreated, respiratory infections can quickly become serious, and can lead to pneumonia or other complications.

There are several things you can do to prevent respiratory infections in your pet rat. First and foremost, it is important to keep your rat's environment clean and dry. Regularly cleaning the cage and providing fresh bedding can help to prevent the growth of bacteria and mold. Avoid using cedar or pine shavings as bedding, as these can be irritating to a rat's respiratory system.

If you notice any symptoms of respiratory infection in your rat, it is important to seek veterinary care right away. Your veterinarian may prescribe antibiotics or other medications to treat the infection. In some cases, supplemental oxygen or nebulizer treatments may be necessary to help your rat breathe more easily. With prompt and appropriate treatment, most respiratory infections can be successfully treated and resolved.

## Tumors

Tumors can be either benign or malignant, and they can develop anywhere on the body. Tumors are caused by uncontrolled cell growth, which results in the formation of a lump or bump.

Benign tumors are non-cancerous and do not spread to other parts of the body. However, they can still cause health problems if they grow too large or press on nearby organs. Malignant tumors, on the other hand, are cancerous and can spread to other parts of the body, making them much more dangerous.

Rats can develop a variety of tumors, including mammary tumors, pituitary tumors, and adrenal gland tumors. Mammary tumors are the most common type of tumor in female rats and can be caused by genetics or hormonal imbalances. Pituitary tumors are often found in older rats and can cause neurological symptoms, such as seizures or loss of balance. Adrenal gland tumors can cause hormonal imbalances and can be accompanied by hair loss or an enlarged abdomen.

Tumors can be treated with surgery or other medical interventions, depending on the size and location of the tumor. It is important to have any new lumps or bumps on your rat checked by a veterinarian as soon as possible, as early detection and treatment can lead to a better outcome.

Mammary tumors;

Most common types of tumors in female rats, and they can be benign or malignant. The exact cause of mammary tumors in rats is unknown, but it is believed to be related to hormonal factors. Mammary tumors usually appear as small, firm, and round lumps under the skin, usually in the area of the mammary glands, which can quickly grow in size and number.

These tumors can affect rats of any age but are more common in older female rats, especially those that have not been spayed. Spaying female rats before the age of six months can reduce the risk of developing mammary tumors. Signs of mammary tumors may include lumps or bumps under the skin, difficulty moving, decreased appetite, lethargy, and weight loss.

If you suspect that your rat has a mammary tumor, you should seek veterinary care as soon as possible. Treatment may involve surgery to remove the tumor or other treatments depending on the severity of the tumor. Early detection and treatment of mammary tumors can increase the chances of a positive outcome.

## Skin

Mites and lice:

There are different types of mites and lice that can infest rats, including fur mites, ear mites, and tropical rat mites. These parasites can cause various skin problems, including irritation, itching, and hair loss.

Infested rats may excessively scratch or bite at their skin, leading to the development of scabs, sores, or crusty patches on their skin. The affected areas may also become red, inflamed, or swollen. If left untreated, mite and lice infestations can worsen and lead to more severe skin problems or secondary infections.

To prevent mite and lice infestations, it is important to keep the rat's living space clean and dry. Regularly cleaning and disinfecting the cage and providing fresh bedding can help prevent infestations. Additionally, treating new rats with a topical parasite treatment and isolating them from other rats for a short period can help prevent the spread of infestations.

If a rat is suspected to have a mite or lice infestation, a veterinarian should be consulted for proper diagnosis and treatment. Treatment usually involves topical or oral medications that are specifically formulated to kill the parasites. In severe cases, additional treatment may be required to address any skin infections or secondary issues caused by the infestation.

Fungal infections;

Are a common skin problem in rats, caused by different types of fungi, including ringworm or dermatitis. These types of infections are contagious and can spread rapidly in a rat colony, as well as to other pets or humans.

Symptoms of fungal infections in rats can include hair loss, redness, itching, and scaly or crusty patches on the skin. The affected area may also be inflamed or appear irritated, and the rat may scratch or bite the affected area in an attempt to relieve the itchiness.

To diagnose a fungal infection, a veterinarian may perform a skin scrape or culture to identify the type of fungus causing the infection. Treatment options typically involve antifungal medications, either topically or orally, depending on the severity and location of the infection.

Preventing fungal infections in rats can be achieved through regular cage cleaning and maintaining good hygiene practices. Infected rats should be isolated and treated promptly to prevent the spread of the infection to other rats or pets in the household. It is also important to keep in mind that some types of fungi that cause skin infections in rats can also affect humans, so proper hygiene and precautionary measures should be taken.

Bacterial infections:

Can be caused by a variety of bacteria such as Staphylococcus aureus, Streptococcus spp., and Pseudomonas aeruginosa, among others. These infections can result from a break in the skin barrier or secondary to other health conditions such as malnutrition or immunosuppression. Symptoms of bacterial skin infections in rats can include redness, swelling, warmth, pus or discharge, and pain or discomfort. In severe cases, the infection can spread to other parts of the body, leading to systemic illness.

Treatment for bacterial skin infections in rats typically involves antibiotics and supportive care. It is important to consult with a veterinarian to determine the appropriate antibiotic regimen and to ensure proper dosage and administration. In some cases, surgical intervention may be necessary to remove infected tissue or to drain abscesses.

Preventing bacterial skin infections in rats involves maintaining good hygiene and providing a clean living environment. This includes regular cleaning of cages and bedding, as well as ensuring rats have access to clean water and a well-balanced diet to maintain optimal health and immunity. It is also important to promptly address any signs of skin irritation or injury to prevent bacteria from entering through the skin.

Allergies:

Are a common problem that affects not only humans but also rats. Domestic rats can develop allergies to different things, such as their bedding materials, food, or environmental factors. The symptoms of allergies in rats can be varied, and it may take some time to identify the cause of the problem.

One of the most common signs of allergies in rats is itching, which can lead to scratching, hair loss, and skin irritation. If the rat is allergic to its bedding material, it may start scratching and rubbing itself against objects, trying to alleviate the itching. In some cases, the rat may develop scabs, sores, or crusty patches on its skin.

Allergies can also cause respiratory problems in rats, such as sneezing, coughing, or wheezing. If the rat is allergic to something in its environment, such as dust or pollen, it may develop these symptoms when exposed to the allergen. In severe cases, allergies can lead to anaphylaxis, a life-threatening reaction that requires immediate veterinary care.

To prevent allergies in rats, it is important to use appropriate bedding materials, feed them a balanced and healthy diet, and keep their environment clean and free of potential allergens. If the rat develops symptoms of an allergic reaction, it is important to take them to a veterinarian for an evaluation and treatment. The veterinarian may recommend antihistamines or other medications to alleviate the symptoms and identify the underlying cause of the problem.

Skin ulcers:

Various factors, can cause skin ulcers such as injuries, bacterial infections, or underlying health issues. They can appear as open sores that do not heal or as raised bumps that may burst and ooze fluid. Ulcers can be painful and may cause discomfort to the rat. They can also be a sign of a more serious health problem, such as malnutrition or immune system disorders. Treatment for skin ulcers in rats typically involves cleaning the affected area and applying topical ointments or antibiotics to prevent further infection. In severe cases, surgery may be necessary to remove infected tissue or to repair the underlying cause of the ulcer.

Skin tutors:

Rats can develop various types of skin tumors, which can be either benign or malignant. Benign tumors are slow-growing and do not usually spread to other parts of the body, whereas malignant tumors can grow quickly and may spread to other organs.

One type of skin tumor that rats can develop is called a fibroma. These are benign tumors that can appear as small, firm lumps on the skin. They are usually harmless, but may need to be removed if they are causing discomfort or affecting the rat's quality of life.

Another type of skin tumor that rats can develop is called a mast cell tumor. These tumors are a type of cancer and can appear as small, round bumps on the skin. They can grow quickly and may spread to other organs, so early diagnosis and treatment are important.

Rats can also develop lipomas, which are benign tumors that form from fat cells. Lipomas can appear as soft, movable lumps under the skin, and are usually harmless. However, they may need to be removed if they are causing discomfort or interfering with the rat's movement.

Other types of skin tumors that rats can develop include sebaceous gland tumors, melanomas, and sarcomas. It is important to monitor any lumps or growths on your rat's skin and to have them checked by a veterinarian if you notice any changes or if they are causing discomfort.

## Bacterial

Bumblefoot:

Also known as pododermatitis. It is a bacterial infection that affects the footpads of rats, causing them to become inflamed, swollen, and painful. The condition is caused by poor living conditions, such as dirty or abrasive cage floors, lack of exercise, and poor diet.

Symptoms of bumblefoot include a swollen, red, or blackened appearance of the footpad, as well as limping or reluctance to move. In severe cases, the footpad may develop a hard, scabby lesion or abscess. Bumblefoot can be painful and can limit a rat's mobility, making it difficult for them to climb or play.

Treatment for bumblefoot usually involves cleaning the affected area, treating any infection with antibiotics, and providing supportive care such as pain management and wound care. Preventative measures such as providing a clean and suitable living environment, a balanced diet, and regular exercise can help reduce the risk of bumblefoot in rats.

Tyzzer's disease:

Is caused by a bacterial organism called Clostridium piliforme. The infection is typically transmitted through ingestion of contaminated food or water, or by direct contact with infected feces.

Symptoms of Tyzzer's disease in rats can include diarrhea, dehydration, lethargy, fever, and weight loss. In severe cases, the infection can lead to liver and heart damage, and can be fatal if left untreated.

Tyzzer's disease is more common in young rats and those with weakened immune systems, such as elderly or sick rats. It is important to seek veterinary care if your rat shows any symptoms of the disease, as early diagnosis and treatment can improve the chances of recovery.

Preventing Tyzzer's disease in rats involves maintaining good hygiene and cleanliness in their living environment, providing clean and fresh water, and avoiding feeding them contaminated food. It is also important to isolate any sick rats from the rest of the colony to prevent the spread of the infection.

Mycoplasma:

This bacteria can be spread easily from rat to rat through direct contact, sneezing, and contaminated bedding or food. Once a rat has been exposed to mycoplasma, they can become a carrier for life.

The bacteria infect the respiratory system of rats and can cause a range of symptoms such as sneezing, coughing, wheezing, and difficulty breathing. The infection can also lead to pneumonia and chronic respiratory disease if left untreated.

Mycoplasma is not curable, but it can be managed with medication and supportive care. Antibiotics such as doxycycline or enrofloxacin can help to control the infection and prevent it from worsening. In severe cases, oxygen therapy or nebulization may be necessary to help the rat breathe more easily.

It is important to note that mycoplasma is highly contagious and can easily spread to other rats in the same environment. If one rat is diagnosed with mycoplasma, it is recommended to isolate them from other rats and thoroughly clean and disinfect their living area to prevent the spread of the bacteria.

Prevention is key when it comes to mycoplasma. Keeping the rat's living area clean and dry, providing good ventilation, and avoiding overcrowding can all help to reduce the risk of infection. Regular check-ups with a veterinarian can also help to catch the infection early and prevent it from progressing.

Bacterial infections:

Can be caused by a variety of bacteria such as Staphylococcus aureus, Streptococcus spp., and Pseudomonas aeruginosa, among others. These infections can result from a break in the skin barrier or secondary to other health conditions such as malnutrition or immunosuppression. Symptoms of bacterial skin infections in rats can include redness, swelling, warmth, pus or discharge, and pain or discomfort. In severe cases, the infection can spread to other parts of the body, leading to systemic illness.

Treatment for bacterial skin infections in rats typically involves antibiotics and supportive care. It is important to consult with a veterinarian to determine the appropriate antibiotic regimen and to ensure proper dosage and administration. In some cases, surgical intervention may be necessary to remove infected tissue or to drain abscesses.

Preventing bacterial skin infections in rats involves maintaining good hygiene and providing a clean living environment. This includes regular cleaning of cages and bedding, as well as ensuring rats have access to clean water and a well-balanced diet to maintain optimal health and immunity. It is also important to promptly address any signs of skin irritation or injury to prevent bacteria from entering through the skin.

## Eyes

Red or swollen eyes:

Eye infections are a common cause of red and swollen eyes in rats. These infections can be caused by bacteria, viruses, or fungi, and can often be treated with antibiotics or antifungal medications.

Allergies can also cause red and swollen eyes in rats. Rats can be allergic to a variety of substances, including bedding materials, food, and environmental irritants like dust and pollen. If an allergy is suspected, it is important to identify and remove the source of the allergen to prevent further symptoms.

In some cases, red or swollen eyes may be a sign of a more serious underlying condition, such as a tumor or abscess near the eye. It is important to have a veterinarian examine the rat if the redness and swelling persist or if there are other accompanying symptoms.

Other symptoms that may accompany red or swollen eyes in rats include discharge from the eye, excessive blinking or squinting, and decreased appetite or lethargy. If any of these symptoms are present, it is important to seek veterinary attention promptly to ensure the best possible outcome for the rat's health.

It is important to monitor your rat's health regularly and seek veterinary care if you notice any signs of illness or health problems.

Cloudy eyes

Cataracts are a common cause of cloudy eyes in older rats, which is a condition that affects the lens of the eye, causing it to become opaque. This can cause a decrease in vision and can eventually lead to blindness.

Cloudy eyes can also be a symptom of an eye infection, such as conjunctivitis or a bacterial infection. These infections can cause inflammation, discharge, and other discomforts in the eyes.

Another possible cause of cloudy eyes in rats is a corneal ulcer. This is an open sore on the surface of the eye that can cause cloudiness, redness, and pain. Corneal ulcers can be caused by injury or trauma to the eye, or by bacterial or fungal infections.

If a rat has cloudy eyes, it is important to take them to a veterinarian for a proper diagnosis and treatment. The vet may perform an eye exam to determine the underlying cause of the cloudiness, and may prescribe eye drops or other treatments to address the issue. In some cases, surgery may be necessary to treat more severe eye problems.

Discharge from the eyes:

Can be a sign of various eye infections, including bacterial, viral, or fungal infections. The discharge can be yellow or green in color and may stick around the rat's eyes or fur. If left untreated, the infection can cause serious eye damage and may even lead to blindness.

Eye discharge can also be a sign of other underlying health issues, such as respiratory infections, allergies, or dental problems. Rats with respiratory infections may experience nasal discharge as well as discharge from their eyes. Allergies can also cause eye discharge in rats, and this can be due to exposure to dust, pollen, or other environmental irritants.

In addition, dental problems such as malocclusion can cause discharge from the eyes in rats. This is because the misalignment of the teeth can cause pressure on the tear ducts, leading to increased tear production and subsequent discharge from the eyes.

If your rat has discharge from the eyes, it is important to take them to a veterinarian as soon as possible. The veterinarian will perform a physical examination and may take samples to determine the cause of the infection. Treatment may involve antibiotics, antiviral or antifungal medications, or other medical interventions depending on the underlying cause of the eye discharge.

Bulging eyes:

Can be a sign of a serious health issue, including an abscess or tumor behind the eye. It can also indicate other health problems, such as hyperthyroidism or a vitamin A deficiency. Bulging eyes may also occur as a result of trauma or injury. If a rat's eyes appear to be bulging, it is important to take the rat to a veterinarian as soon as possible. The vet will perform a thorough examination to determine the cause of the bulging eyes and recommend the appropriate treatment. Treatment may include antibiotics, surgery, or other medical interventions depending on the underlying cause. Ignoring this symptom can lead to serious complications and can even be life-threatening for the rat.

Swollen eyelids:

One of the common causes of swollen eyelids is a blocked tear duct. The tear ducts in rats can become blocked due to an infection or inflammation, leading to a build-up of tears in the tear ducts and swelling of the eyelids. This can cause discomfort to the rat and may require veterinary treatment.

Swollen eyelids can also be a sign of an abscess or infection, particularly if the swelling is accompanied by redness or discharge. Abscesses can occur anywhere on the body and may require surgical intervention to remove the pus-filled pocket.

Another potential cause of swollen eyelids in rats is allergies. Just like humans, rats can develop allergies to certain substances, such as bedding materials, food, or dust. If the swelling is accompanied by itching or other signs of an allergic reaction, it is important to identify and remove the allergen to prevent further health issues.

In some cases, swollen eyelids can be a sign of more serious health issues such as tumors or cancer. These conditions can cause the eyelids to become inflamed and may require immediate veterinary attention.

It is important to monitor your rat's eyes regularly and seek veterinary care if you notice any swelling, redness, or discharge. Early detection and treatment of eye issues can help prevent further complications and maintain your rat's overall health and well-being.

## 22. Preventing health issues

Preventing health issues in rats involves several factors, including proper nutrition, hygiene, and environmental management. Here are some tips to help prevent health issues in rats:

1. Provide a balanced diet: Rats require a diet that is high in protein and low in fat. Feed them a diet that is specifically formulated for rats, and avoid giving them high-calorie or sugary foods.

2. Maintain good hygiene: Keep the rat's living area clean and free of waste, food, and bedding debris. Regularly clean the cage, toys, and accessories with mild soap and water.

3. Provide plenty of fresh water: Rats need access to clean water at all times. Change their water daily and clean the water bottle or bowl regularly.

4. Monitor for signs of illness: Check your rat's eyes, nose, ears, and skin for signs of infection or illness. Monitor their behavior, appetite, and energy levels for any changes.

5. Handle your rat regularly: Rats are social animals and require regular interaction with their owners. Handling them regularly can help identify health issues early and reduce stress.

6.Provide a comfortable living environment: Make sure the cage is appropriately sized, with enough space for the rats to move around comfortably. Provide plenty of toys and activities to keep them mentally stimulated.

7. Avoid overcrowding: Rats can become stressed if they are overcrowded, which can lead to health issues. Provide enough space for each rat to have their own sleeping area and avoid keeping too many rats together in one cage.

## 23. Spaying and neutering

Spaying and neutering are common procedures performed on rats to prevent unwanted litters and to address certain health and behavioral issues. These procedures are typically performed by a veterinarian under general anesthesia.

Spaying female rats can help prevent uterine infections, mammary tumors, and ovarian cysts, as well as reduce the risk of developing certain reproductive cancers. It can also help reduce aggressive behavior in some rats and prevent unwanted breeding.

Neutering male rats can help prevent testicular tumors, reduce aggressive behavior, and prevent unwanted breeding. It can also help reduce the risk of certain types of prostate problems.

It is important to consult with a veterinarian to determine the appropriate age for spaying or neutering your rat. In general, rats can be spayed or neutered as early as 3 to 6 months of age. After the procedure, it is important to monitor your rat closely for any signs of discomfort or complications, and follow any post-operative care instructions provided by your veterinarian.

## 24. Breeding

Breeding rats can be a fun and rewarding experience, but it is important to have a thorough understanding of the process and responsibilities that come with it. In this chapter, we will discuss the basics of breeding rats, including preparation, breeding techniques, and care for the offspring.

Breeding rats requires a good understanding of their reproductive cycle. Female rats typically reach sexual maturity between 5-6 weeks of age, while male rats may become sexually mature around 8-10 weeks of age. However, it is best to wait until both rats are at least 4-6 months old before breeding them, to ensure they are fully developed and healthy.

Rats are polyestrous, meaning they can go into heat every 4-5 days if they do not mate. During heat, the female rat will exhibit signs such as restlessness, increased activity, increased vocalization and an arching of the back.

It is essential to note that male rats may also become more aggressive during this time, so it is important to introduce them carefully and supervise the mating process.

When breeding rats, it is important to introduce them slowly and carefully to avoid any injuries or aggressive behavior. It is best to place the female rat in the male's cage, as this will reduce any territorial behavior. It is also important to supervise the mating process to ensure that both rats are mating correctly and to avoid any injuries.

After the successful mating, the female rat will undergo gestation for approximately 21-23 days, during which she will require a quiet and stress-free environment. As the due date approaches, it is essential to prepare a clean and comfortable nesting area for the mother rat to give birth. The nesting area should be spacious enough to accommodate the mother rat and her litter and should be lined with soft bedding materials such as shredded paper or cloth.

Once the pups are born, it is crucial to handle them with care and avoid any stress to the mother rat and her litter. The pups are born blind, hairless, and entirely dependent on their mother for food and warmth. The mother rat will produce milk to feed her litter, and it is essential to ensure that she has adequate food and water during this time. It is also recommended to provide her with high-quality protein-rich food to support milk production and her overall health.

As the pups grow and develop, it is important to monitor their health and growth. Regular checkups with a veterinarian are recommended to ensure that they are healthy and free of any illnesses or infections. Once the pups reach 4-6 weeks of age, they can be weaned and separated from their mother. At this point, it is crucial to provide them with a suitable and spacious living environment and a balanced diet to support their growth and development.

## 25. Looking after the pups

Keep them warm:

Keeping rat pups warm is essential for their survival and proper development. Rat pups are born naked, blind, and unable to regulate their body temperature. They rely on their mother for warmth and nourishment for the first few weeks of their lives.

To keep rat pups warm, it is essential to maintain a warm and draft-free environment. The nesting area should be kept at a temperature between 75-85°F. You can use a heat lamp or a heating pad to maintain the temperature. The heat source should be placed at one end of the nesting area, so the rat pups can move away from it if they become too hot. It is crucial to monitor the temperature regularly to ensure that it remains stable and within the recommended range.

It is also essential to provide adequate bedding material for the pups to snuggle into for warmth. Soft and absorbent materials, such as shredded paper, cloth, or fleece, can be used. The bedding should be changed regularly to maintain cleanliness and hygiene.

If the mother rat is absent or unable to provide warmth to the pups, you can use a surrogate heat source. A warm water bottle wrapped in a towel or a heating pad set on low can provide the necessary warmth. It is important to ensure that the heat source is not too hot and that the rat pups have enough space to move away from it if needed.

Proper warmth is critical to the health and development of rat pups. By providing a warm and comfortable environment, you can help ensure their well-being and increase their chances of survival.

Provide adequate nutrition:

Rat pups rely on their mother's milk for the first few weeks of life. Ensure that the mother rat has access to plenty of food and water to produce enough milk. Additionally, provide high-quality rat food to the mother rat to maintain her health and nutrition.

If a mother rat is not feeding her pups, there could be a few different reasons. Some possible causes include illness or injury in the mother rat, a lack of milk production, or rejection of the litter. If you notice that the mother rat is not feeding her pups, it's important to take action quickly to ensure their survival.

Here are some steps you can take if the mother rat isn't feeding her pups:

Check the mother rat's health: If the mother rat is sick or injured, she may not be able to nurse her pups. Look for signs of illness or injury, such as lethargy, loss of appetite, or wounds. If you suspect that the mother rat is sick or injured, contact a veterinarian for advice.

Supplement the pups' diet: If the mother rat isn't producing enough milk, you may need to supplement the pups' diet with formula. There are commercial formulas available at pet stores, or you can make your own formula using a recipe recommended by a veterinarian.

Hand-rear the pups: If the mother rat rejects her litter, you may need to hand-rear the pups. This involves feeding them with a syringe or bottle every few hours and providing them with a warm, clean nesting area. Hand-rearing can be time-consuming and challenging, but it's necessary to ensure the pups' survival.

Foster the pups: If you're unable to care for the pups yourself, you can try to find a foster mother rat to nurse them. This can be done by introducing the pups to a mother rat who has recently given birth or is lactating.

Keep the nest clean:

Keeping the nesting area clean is crucial for the health and wellbeing of rat pups. The mother rat will naturally keep the nest clean by removing any soiled bedding or waste produced by the pups, but it is also essential to provide regular cleaning to ensure that the environment remains sanitary.

The frequency of cleaning will depend on the size of the litter and how quickly they produce waste. In general, it is recommended to clean the nest every 2-3 days. This involves removing all the soiled bedding and replacing it with fresh, clean bedding material. Be sure to use bedding material that is safe for the pups and their mother, such as shredded paper or aspen shavings, and avoid using materials like cedar or pine, which can be harmful to rats.

When cleaning the nesting area, it is also important to keep the pups warm and avoid stressing them or their mother. Try to clean the area when the mother rat is out of the nest or distracted with food. You can use a small spoon or scoop to remove soiled bedding, being careful not to disturb the pups too much. Once the bedding is removed, add fresh, clean bedding and smooth it down to create a comfortable and secure nest for the pups.

It is important to monitor the cleanliness of the nest regularly and to be vigilant for any signs of illness or infection in the pups. If you notice any unusual behavior or symptoms, such as lethargy, loss of appetite, or diarrhea, contact a veterinarian immediately for advice and treatment.

Handling:

When handling rat pups, it is important to be gentle and avoid any sudden movements or loud noises. Always approach them slowly and with caution, so as not to startle them or cause unnecessary stress. You should also make sure your hands are clean and free of any strong scents, such as perfume or soap, which could upset the mother rat and her litter.

It is essential to limit handling of rat pups until they are at least 10-14 days old, as they are very fragile and can easily become injured. Once they are a bit older, you can handle them briefly, but always with care and attention. When picking them up, gently scoop them up with both hands, supporting their entire body, and avoid holding them by their tail or limbs.

It is also important to remember that rat pups have very delicate respiratory systems, so it is crucial to avoid exposing them to any irritants or pollutants, such as cigarette smoke or cleaning chemicals. Keep their environment clean and well-ventilated, and avoid exposing them to any potential hazards or dangers.

Monitoring the growth and development:

Is essential to ensure their well-being and catch any potential health problems early. Here are some ways to monitor their growth and development:

Weigh the pups regularly: It's important to weigh the pups daily or every few days to ensure that they are gaining weight at a healthy rate. Use a small kitchen scale or a postal scale to weigh them. Rat pups should gain about 2-3 grams per day.

Check for any abnormalities: Inspect the pups daily for any abnormalities, such as wounds, discharge, or signs of illness. If you notice any signs of illness or poor growth, seek veterinary care immediately.

Observe their behavior: Monitor the pups' behavior and make sure they are active, nursing frequently, and behaving normally. Rat pups should be active and curious, and they should be nursing frequently from their mother.

Track their milestones: Rat pups develop quickly, and it's important to track their milestones. For example, they should open their eyes by day 14 and start exploring their environment by day 21. Keep a record of when these milestones occur to ensure that the pups are developing normally.

Socialization: As the rat pups grow, it's important to provide them with socialization opportunities. Handle them gently and encourage interaction with their littermates and with humans. Socialization can help them become well-adjusted and friendly rats as they mature.

By monitoring the growth and development of rat pups, you can ensure that they are healthy and well-cared for. If you have any concerns about the pups' health or growth, don't hesitate to seek veterinary care.

Weaning:

Is the process of gradually transitioning them from their mother's milk to solid food. Rat pups should be weaned at around 3-4 weeks of age. Here are some tips on how to wean rat pups properly:

Introduce solid food gradually: Start by offering small amounts of solid food, such as high-quality rat food or soft foods like mashed vegetables. At first, the pups may not be interested in the solid food, but encourage them to try it by placing it in their cage. Gradually increase the amount of solid food offered over a period of several days.

Offer fresh water: As the pups begin to eat solid food, it's essential to provide them with fresh water. Offer water in a shallow dish or water bottle, making sure it's easily accessible to the pups.

Monitor their intake: Keep an eye on the pups' food and water intake to ensure that they are eating and drinking enough. If you notice any changes in their appetite or behavior, it may be a sign of illness or other health issues.

Continue to provide milk: Even as the pups begin to eat solid food, they will still nurse from their mother. Gradually reduce the amount of nursing sessions until they are fully weaned. It's important not to separate the pups from their mother too soon, as they still need her care and socialization.

Remove the mother rat: Once the pups are fully weaned, it's time to remove the mother rat from the cage. This can be done gradually by separating her from the pups for a few hours each day until they are completely independent.

## 26. Conclusion

Owning a rat can offer a plethora of benefits beyond just being a cute and cuddly pet. Rats are intelligent creatures that can learn to do tricks and even respond to their names. They are also social animals that enjoy interacting with their owners and other rats. With proper care and training, rats can become beloved members of the family. Rats also have a fascinating history in science and medicine, and continue to play an important role in research. Additionally, rats are low-maintenance pets that require minimal space and can fit into a variety of lifestyles. Despite their negative reputation as pests, rats are gaining recognition as wonderful pets that can bring joy and companionship to their owners. If you are considering a new pet, a rat may be a great choice for those seeking a unique and rewarding pet ownership experience.

Printed in Great Britain
by Amazon